'Lil

Bits of

Life

BY JORDAN WATSON

Published by:
Maximized Productions, UPH Div.
6715 Suitland Road
Morningside, Maryland 20746
1 (301) 420-1460
www.maximizedproductions.com
ISBN: 979-8-9991703-0-9 Paperback
ISBN: 979-8-9991703-1-6 Hardback

Printed in the United States of America 2025

This manuscript is presented with the understanding that the author and publisher are not engaged in rendering legal advice, counsel, or financial or professional advice. The author and publisher especially disclaim any liability that is incurred from the use of these poems, prayers, and all information provided, and from the application of the contents of this book in its entirety.

CONTENTS

CONTENTS

Dedication:

God

and

My Beloved Parents

Thank You's:

BCB, George, Summer, Halo, Lil' one, Coco, Bubbie, Delta, Needles

MUSIC

You do inspire us so to go on and to strive
Where there seems to be no strength to push
on to where we do not know to go

The melodies so pleasing, sometimes teasing,
Not always for our reasoning

Oh, to give us calm by such a sound
The many journeys you take through our minds,
So many times in a cappella, you compel us to reach
ranges of our minds, we dare not tread alone.

Old time record tunes stream in, we respond
Again and again to your blends

The light you bring within sing

BURSTING BUBBLES

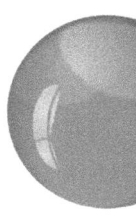

Colors shoot forth
They swirl, circle, alight
Delightful pockets of air
Breezing on summertime winds

Some come gushing, gushing forth
Others gently saunter their way
Gliding, bursting just as they touch
The memories of humanities hope

The bravery of adventure
The desire of flight and feeling the heart of
I wish I might, I wish I might

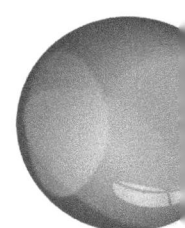

Soar and reach the skies of my mind
Sing with the words of childhood stingingly, clinging
to the purities of freedom

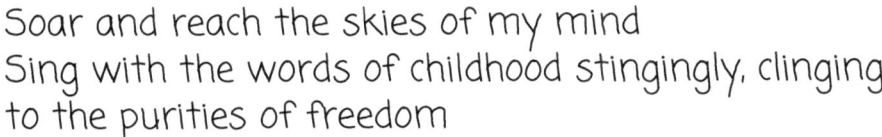

try with earthbound wings
try jump, then stumble
run, run, start, start again, stumble
I wish I might, I wish I might

Wings of dreams come true
imbue these limbs toward celestial heights
I want to spin a star tonight
I want to fly
I wish I might, I wish I might

Rest beside the bubble's door
and catch a spatial ride
Inside or out, just before it dissipates
And I fall, fall, fall amidst space

Come catch the contagion
While childhood lingers here
I wish I might, I wish I might

BEAST AMONG US

Go ahead say your name
We know who you are
Its too late to keep silent
You have been identified, by all that you do

Bumping people hard with your shoulder
Disrespecting the shy, quiet and independent
Yes we know who you are, but do you know
You could be something other than what you are

You could be enjoyed and appreciated
Even love could announce itself to you
However, your name keeps emerging
Explore your depths to discover

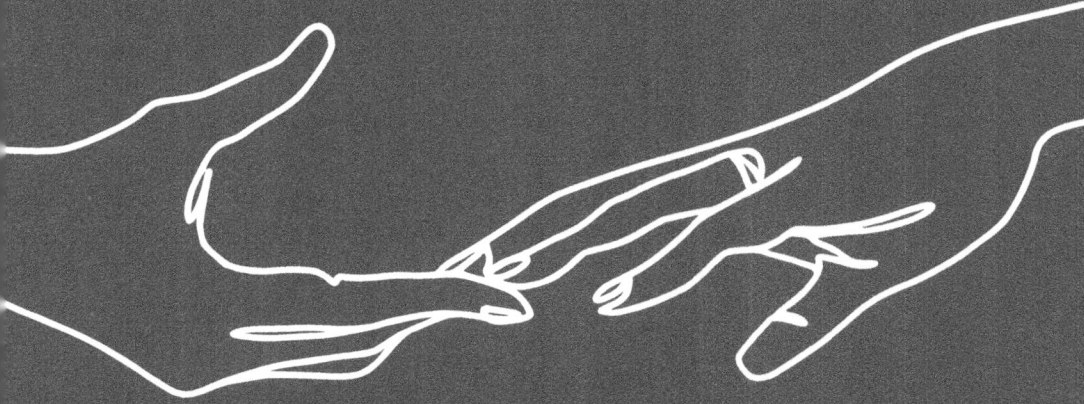

04

Solitude allows a quiet place to relate to yourself
Honor truths only you acknowledge
Forgive unkindness to provide acceptance
Bring lots of laughter back and
let your side hurt from it
Put the smile not just on the lips,
but in the eyes and heart

Deep breaths straighten the back
Integrity straightens the spine
Joy seeps in and suddenly
You are recognized

Guess who you see, not just the welcoming world
Family, friends, associates, acquaintances, strangers
A familiar soul, once apart and lonely
Now warmly engaging, sharing in life
Thirstily living because old queries are answered
Peace pushes through, Now

You recognize You

05

BIRDS EYE VIEW

Flutter, Flutter
He won't let me go.
Flutter, Flutter
He's never been free, so how can he possibly free me.

I don't want seeds again!
I'd much prefer to dine out tonight. He does not understand
my plight.
Flutter, Flutter

TAKE MY WINGS THEN!
and let me sit here, as you do now
Then, as you do, I should begin the next most natural sequence.
I should use my mind.

If I begin to use my mind, I might begin to do, as you have done.
I might think to catch a being of flight, like a bumble bee.
And sit him in a cage, as you have done me
And then, I might take his wings away; And then he might begin to
think. . .As I have done. . .and dream the dreams of NO! NO!

GIVE ME MY DAMN wings back. . .Flutter, Flutter

LIFE

Crawling, toddling, walking, running
tri-a-cycles, bi-a-cycles
jet machines, up-a-way-things,
noise-a-mobiles,
speed 45 miles an hour, 75 miles, 120 miles an hour
tick tock clocks, pace maker machines,
a million things to do,
24 hours in everyday
racing, pacing, going here and there, everywhere
from the womb we go, into the tomb we go
life is death, death is life.

GLOVES UP

The brutality of a boxing ring
All sense has left the mind
Blood is flowing, eyes are bruised
Strong bodies deliberately collide

While they prance the dance of violence
Force takes its place and humanity fades
Man's animalistic thirst takes its place, as king
No victors here tonight or any night

Though ferocity takes a seat in each corner
A splash of water til the bell rings again
The slow dance of battle with cunning looks
gloves up, swing, swing, body blows and pain

A jab here, a jab there, now locked in a violent embrace.
Power risk the life of two engaging in a tiresome prance
The referee separating the entangled, exhausted two
Power hungry beasts determined to define man

One in blue and white, the other in black and red
Blood streaming from both heads, arms up, bounce
fake a swing, then swing, slow, slow and backward and
forward, pace

More water in the corners, bell rings, come out swinging

Working the midsection, back bent on the ropes.
Separation, back on the ropes, separation, a little bounce, a little
swing, more fight, more swing.
How on earth do we end this thing?
Man's desire to dominate is in the ring. One man slips to a knee.
Up again in this final round, declaring no winner to be found.

ONE

HE leads/ SHE follows
He looks back towards/ Her face

SHE frowns/ HE stands still
HE holds his breath/ SHE Waits

SHE smiles/ HE sighs

SHE looks into/ HIS eyes
HE extends a hand backward to/ HER

HE waits for/ HER grasp instead/ SHE dances

SHE dances seductively and slow
SHE creates a rhythm's river

THEY flow
THEY mesh

TWO lead
TWO grow

LOVE

I like the love I see
When he was young, he discovered
the word metamorphosis
He walked around the stores and said
to me, ooh, mommy all these toys are
causing a metamorphosis in me

He is adored
his company is sought constantly
there is quiet inside
people sense that

people like quiet
its calming

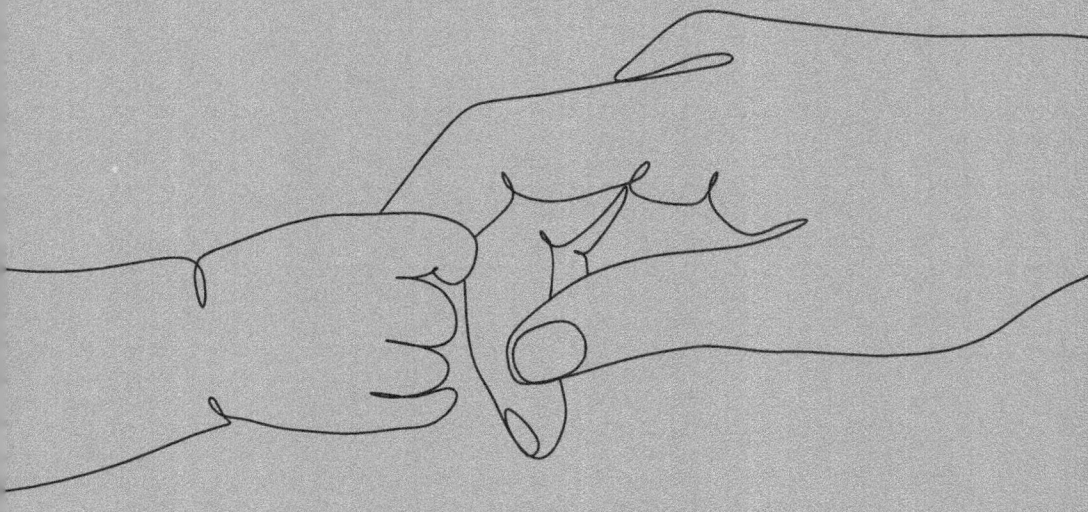

I like the love I see
moms taking their boys and girls into the ladies public
restroom teaching little ones not to touch the seat
don't peek at other people
wash your hands
soap once, rub twice, rinse and dry

I like the love I see
Look around, it still abounds
a sister telling a brother to be careful
not to stick himself with a tiny wire tie

I like the love I see
A mother willing to travel across the world
to help her only child grow academically
A mother giving her life savings to support
a daughter irrespective of the costs

I like the love I see

Here come the LOUD UMS

Here come the LOUD UMS
They bring with them plenty of fun and a great deal of noise
You know they're coming because they arrive before they get there
They always announce themselves to everyone nearby and those far away
You can be busy applying yourself to any task at hand only to be shocked into distraction

All this noise is generally because of a great discussion or possibly an argument
Hopefully its for the former rather than vice versa and usually accompanied by merriment
Though merriment is not alone, it comes with warm, friendly, lighthearted people

People who thrive on their comradability with each other or combustibility depending on the subject

Loud ums can't just break a plate or stumble downstairs, their actions must be accompanied with ooohs or aaahs then their laughter which equals surround sound
Giggles heightened into the call of the hyena
While tears emerge in silence, frowned faces come with wails of woes, two maybe three times
Stumblers tumbling involves the colliding of friends who boisterously complain into blames of
Who was first, then the last to clash all becomes a clatter as to what was in fact the real matter
Which was to cause such delight which enriched the life of all who were around to engage in the many sounds of the Loud ums

Game time is quite simply an excuse to kick up ones feet, rare back in a chair, hunch your seat mate and cackle only to repeat what both have witnessed
All this leads to more ooohs and aaahs, pointed fingers, loud knee slappings and hand clappings for sure

By any chance, were you one of the many who participated in such an event because rumor has it, that you were very definitely there somewhere in all this calamity of merriment and stunned fun

Were you there? Are you a card carrying member of the Loud Ums? Rumor has it, that they all look alike you know. Don't believe it, just take a peek and see who you spy, go ahead all it takes is a curious eye, an honest ear and you will be able to identify this rowdy bunch.

Hey, some days, they often even sit together for lunch.

BUMPING INTO YOU

I met a fellow traveler today
we smiled for a ...moment
and looked each others way.

Unknown spirits with similar thoughts
We feel at home, social,
not alone, anymore.

Listening, caring, sharing
The deeply arcane is whispered

Condemnation haunts the bus,
Eyes speak, sighs confirm;

One with another spirit.
There are two of us, now.

Two for a. . .moment.

　　Signed
　　Warmed inside and quiet

NEW LIFE

The Lightning flashes in and out of my soul
In and out of our lives bringing the storms
in between the mundane existences that occur
and the sparks fly infrequently but just as startlingly

Nature's strength reminds us of the fragility of life
So quickly a bolt of lightning split the redwood tree
While the morning kisses the tulip and daffodil with dew
tiny specks of dust whirlwind into a blinding dry twister

Rivers flow from droplets emerging from clouds above
Rendering waters to quench any animals thirst
Providing transport safely here and there
Flooding out riverbanks and adjusting landscapes

Then once again creating serene and still sunsets
Picturesque locales inspire the brush of many a painter
To capture the beauty of a flowers petal
Teaching us to appreciate beauty while respecting nature

Natures song always has an illusive rhythm
Never the same but always perfect in its delivery
freshly reminding us of its gentle nurturing ways
Teasing, taunting then bursting forth with new life

FIVE MINUTES TOO . . .

Backpack on the right shoulder
Headphones circle neck
Jacket under left arm
Phone in right hand
Croissant in mouth
Hair is mussed
Left hand pulling up back of pants

Late to school, class, and practice
Can't find clean socks,
assignments or report cards
Hearing impaired
Teeth in braces
Wearing $800 sneakers

Game master and defender of right
Entitled pretentious attitude with adults
Eight hundred friends via social media
Although, easily punked online and in person
by shadowy, cowardly bullacious people

SENSES

All kinds of thoughts come to mind
when I think of how pleasant life can be;

    a touch that is a dream
    a song evolving from a whisper
    joy from a smile
    laughter from my own heart beat

Perhaps all is premature
And yet it is slow and yearns for more.

WEE HOURS

In the wee hours of the morning
Sun is barely just up
The room is still
Sound waves music the ear

There is ubiquitous quiet
A smile from within emerges
Still waters deeply stir the soul
Peace reins in the heart

Eyes search through the calm
Drinking in the solitude of each moment
Clinging stickily to every illusive second
Wanting to keep it in place for a lifetime

A lifetime of tranquil troubleless events
Full of the best of the beautiful
Sweetest unperturbed existences
Transcending into what we call

Day after day after day,
Life

THE WIND

You ever watch the wind rustle the leaves of a tree on
a warm summer day
Its like God is talking to you at the same time cause
you can feel the hairs on your arm
as he blows his breath
Its like watching a newborn smile or coo softly

I like listening to children outside my window
their laughter is music to my heart
Their laughter gives the memory of yesterday
It reminds me of that day when we used to play
And for a semi second I am back there

out of breath, panting needing some water to refresh
and begin again to run, run, run

delight at butterflies, fall in the grass
catch fireflies in a jar, and sing
oh mary mack, mack, mack
red light, green light

Blowing bubbles, jumping rope, hopscotch
Step on a crack..

Even the silence is precious
Mmmm listen you can almost hear a breeze
A breeze of fun, joy, peace, life

ROSE DUST

While you can't tolerate others
We have to stomach you and all your insensitivities
to people who are different from you
and lets face it everyone is different from you
No one is going to be like you and really, thank goodness too

A miserable soul
finds a speck of disgust on a rose
Rainbows are formed from dust particles,
moisture and solar light
Rain is an imposition although it nourishes the
earth and its inhabitants

Heck babies are irritating and plain ole
bothersome rather than a joy
soft is too soft, hard is impenetrable, the wind
musses the hair

Blue is not blue enough, Cats smell, Dogs do too
Lets not begin to focus on people, we might find
something wrong with them
Despite the fact that many of them are
energetic, warm and happy

A miserable soul
finds a speck of disgust on a rose

20

WARMTH
SALE

Warmth for sale
What price will you pay
We have a special today

If you feel chilly, come our way
Our specialty is chasing chill bumps
Though they like to pop up here and there
We managed to get them on the move

Our intent is to offer the best quality of titillating tingles
to each and every chilly bump

Yep warmth for sale
We believe the price is right
So, if you have a bump that wants to purchase the glow
Please let one or more of our representatives know While
this offer is quite appealing
The offer is fleeting, so purchased quickly
Glows have to worry about overheating and/or chilling out

Warmth for sale
The price is right, right now
Don't be the last to feel this incredible sensory delight
Where tingles abound only momentarily
Chasing away cold skin prickles into moments of Aaaaah..

TWIN POPS

Sharing is something you learn in childhood

If you miss that boat, it colors the rest of your life.

I didn't think about this until the memories of twin pops came to mind.

I don't know about you, but my favorite was orange creamsickles.

Popsickle twin pops were my alternative enjoyment, how bout you?

I remember trying to hurry up and decide, if I wanted to break it first, lick it a little

then break it before it started dripping and I had to bend over to keep it from dripping on my pretty, white shorts and culottes.

I, also, remember on the hottest days being so happy that first there was

One, then thinking I got two all to myself and relishing in satisfaction.

But sometimes, being so focused on my two til a friend comes up

and has the nerve to ask me to do the ultimate.

And that's when their friendship comes into question, cause would a true friend ask?

Suddenly, I can remember all the bad things they did or didn't do to or with me.

Next my greed comes into play, if I don't share, will they remember me when I need it.

Did my mother say to share or not to share? I am willing to defer to my mother said, no!

BUUUUU-UUUUUUT, she didn't say that, so I can't use her, as an escape.

I am remembering that I didn't ask others to share their twin pops because... I just didn't.

Was it because I didn't want to share or empathy, not so sure now.

My friend says, that's why I don't eat twin pops, I had to share with my sister

So would you share your twin pop with me, Slurp?

SONG

A Song evolving from a whisper

Joy from a smile

You know I see you want to smile, go head let it go wild
I mean what would it hurt to know you rather laugh a
little while
rather than find a problem, cause you know you got to
solve 'em

Girl, you know you want to smile, go head let it go wild
a little baby going down the sliding board for its first ride
Letting out a surprised squeal of delight brings a smile
from deep inside
Making you remember the joy of that glide

Mmmm hmmm
Did you notice the bright, colorful hues after a summer
rain
Or the many pretty umbrellas walking in the streets
trying to avoid the drops
Just drop the umbrellas, look up into the sky and feel the
wind and rain in your face
Cause when you're wet and your hair has been exposed
you know you might as well go wild and let out that smile

24

Bake some cookies with your family
Make the whole house smell good with vanilla
Let your senses breathe in the aroma of the sweetness in the air
Laugh and joke around, let your ribcage jiggle from the warmth
of camaraderie

And when that timer dings, all eyes twinkle
the inner smile peers outwardly a little
Everyone rushes in for their first taste
Mmmm hmmm
You know you want to smile, go head let it go wild
Its going around, watch the count, this thing is
contagious Its exhilarating, its spirit filled, its a great
goodness
Its worth the wild, go head go on and smile
Yeah smile, go on and smile

SNOWFLAKES

The music of the snowflakes is a
crinkle of cold dust swirling in the air
Its promised of the cleansing purity
floating, guiding ever so gently
allowing us to witness its flight until
it lands glisteningly on blades of grass
and
mountain tops, barbed wire, fences,
and
skyscrapers, rooftops, dusty planes,
and
trucks, cars, the family dog, buses, and
us.

Our eye rises towards the sky and
our noses crinkle and our smiles open up
and a memory tingles inside of
squeals of delight from falling into
snowy piles of the fresh soft stuff to
mama's making ice cream from it and
dads, boys, and girls shoveling it with
smiles on their faces to building snowmen
and eventually ice structures

the music of the snowflakes is the crinkle of cold white purified
dust creating in us good times of laughter, fun, love, joy
with flakes of mommy, daddy, brother, sister, family, neighbors,
community sprinkled into good times to be shared and warm,
glowing fireplace to invite us in from the snowflakes embrace,
so we can gaze outside our window at the landscapes new and
ever so changing view where we see icicles hanging from rooftops
people bundled up with hats, scarves, gloves, and mitten
reminding us to love to warms embrace now, because we
danced in the colds grace and played with its musical swirls
of affection, allowing us to willingly compose any, and every
whim from his descending flight of light collections interrupting
our worlds of work and solitude to remember freedom voice
within each of us, individually, and collectively, the snowflakes
emerge both above and within ever so gently floating out our
dust of pure creativity to speak as individually as a snowflake

27

SCAREDY CAT

I been scared my whole life
Tired of it
First just scared of dogs,
til the cats taught me the same thing, too

Scared of people judging everything
My smile and that I don't do it enough
the way I hold my head
my walk
my speech pattern
I don't speak loud enough
I shouldn't speak until spoken to
unless its morning when I better speak to you

Scared of men because I don't know them
Scared of women because they want to prove they are as
tough as men
Scared guys won't like me
Scared they will like me too much

Scared of the boss
coworkers
the public
new ideas
new inventions
young people
bullies and they are everywhere

Scared of life in general
Not scared of death yet though
maybe when its time
but if I think about life
I might just jump in with relish and a hotdog

I'm tired of being scared

Tit for Tat

You do this and I'll do that
It interferes with love of all kinds

I got your this and I got your that
Cause if you don't do this for me
Then I won't do that for you

I'm not feeling the love
I'm feeling the hate

Tit for Tat should be reversed to
Tat for Tit

If, I wash your car today
You can wash mine tomorrow

I bake you a cake
You bake me a pie

When I am low
You bring me up high

I think I like Tat for Tit
much more than Tit for Tat

Can you get with that?

SOPPER'S DELIGHT

MMMmm Not just any cuisine will do
Truly mouth watering memories
which have defined my physical girth
sad to say, it was earned this way

Have you ever tasted a hot biscuit,
smeared with melted butter
oooh on a plate with warm syrup
talk about a sopper's delight

Some folks like biscuits and gravy
and use a knife and fork
to cut, lift, chew and swallow
A mundane though sophisticated approach

Grasping a nice hot biscuit
while your eyes savour a smile of its own
anticipating the sensations, the tongue waters
fingers ready that biscuit piece

to dip and swirl, savour and taste
thats how I spiral the food on my plate
but to be honest, I don't waste my time
the food I eat must be divine

No I don't sop for any old treat
this wrist only twist for the worthiest
Potato salad, beans and greens
Warm cornbread, mashed potatoes and stringbeans
the mouth opens as the tongue receives
like the wide receiver twisting a pretty mid-air catch
ball received and delivery executed

This is how I sop, so let me sop
there is no sweeter gift to the lips
Oh yeah, I said it
Its the kind that makes
your mouth water when
you remember that plate and also the
reason why you walk with that gait
The best food initiates the swirl
the impulsive twist of the fingers
to clean the plate of any remnant of delight
irrespective of the cuisine

How do you sop your food?
do you get your fingers wet, if so
you are a sloppy eater
and don't qualify as a sopper

Sopper's finish off their meal
by cleaning their plate
Oh they are having discussions,
laughing, talking to others but
their primary focus is sopping
every morsel on that plate

ROLLER COASTER

Goes up and down
Round and whirling round
No stops, some lunges
Plenty of startling hair raising plunges

Wavering spirals on a man made trap
Scintillate each nerve ending with a zap
Sagacious turns delight the mind
Establishing fright one more time

Fun filled curves of sheer joy
Hosting laughter in its roar
Arms way up, if you dare
Ubiquitous arms everywhere

The physics of nature enables this ride
The fastest locked down motorized slide!
Momentum building on every slope
Promising to deliver a top speed jolt

Roller coaster, the ride
Roller coaster, the slide
High flying twisted flips
Spend your money, take a trip

Chill bumps pop up the arm
the heart races with the sound of this
mesmerizing traveling dare
Roller coastering people everywhere

We-e-e-e, giggle with excitement
We-e-e-e laugh to the extreme
Scream - scream - scream
Yell and pray
We-e-e love this kind of play

33

JASMINE

The daily sunrise offers a
Rainbow of beautiful hopes
round, rosy cheeks with
ebullient, new cheerful
energy sources of light

The pure beauty
of life and belief
dream a dream of wonder
adventure without fear

laughter in the tummy
joy quickly appears
pitter patter little feet
running stumbling

glimpsing
understanding
evolving with growth
ambling on my way

loving with honesty
accepting all kindness
brown, blue, grey, green eyes
look on to recognition

of all thats offered freely
tasting sweet treats cause
lifting eyebrows to join the
slow emerging smile

of a child

GOOSE BUMP ENDINGS

A husband and wife and the emergence of their
new born baby Struggling, striving and then success

A young boys football team being hurt and sacked
repeatedly yet ultimately triumphs
They limp off the field having lost
but hearts still soar because there
is still hope

A little one falls and hurts their knee or elbow
Mom or dad arrives and picks the little one up
takes them home, cleans the wound, sanitizes it
bandaids the scrape, wipes the tear, kisses the forehead
hugs their child and checks to make sure the love is felt
silent courage acknowledged
one heart smiled,
the other is soothed you decide which is which

the first short term goodbyes
first day of kindergarten, camp, middle
school, college, marriage

Hard fought battles against
bullies, facts of life, dashed crushes,
first true loves

A warm buttered croissant

35

LEMONADE ZEST

The noise is inside
Its constant, too
It won't let me sleep either

I like to feel quiet, sometimes on the inside
Don't feel it enough, though

I like it because it reminds me of
lemonade made just right
not too sweet and seedless
nothing to interrupt the gulp or
strangle the swirling taste
of fresh lemon meat floating in waves
over the crackling ice promising to stymie
the heat of a ninety degree day

producing repetitive smiles inside
claiming the day without speaking
catching a breeze when there isn't one
and holding true to who I am

only one in nature
surely God's child, too
among the delights of Arizona marbling orange
and white sunrises
and white Atlantic waves slushing ashore
gifts remind the mind
calm the energy source
to come on and rock me, rock me back to sleep
with life's rhythm to rejuvenate and exhilarate
tomorrow's day

EVERY PAINT STROKE

Music of the stroke
Take up the brush, swirl it into the paint
There is even rhythm in the prep of coloration

flowing free on canvas
Speaking without words
feeling the heart of ones soul

Expressing one's spirit
an in depth analysis of the moments flow
driven by the inner speak and adhering to its know
Its one sided conversation must be acknowledged
whether understood or not, revelation is the key

ebb, movement and flow like that on the ocean's floor
emerges atop and onto lands shore, speaking with its only voice

Whether understood or not, but felt yes because
the kiss of the soul is and must be memorable because
its voice constantly echoes, echoes, I am here
I exist, exist, exist, Remember me, always, always, because
my voice may be quieted, it may be silenced but it never leaves
until the carrier leaves and even then it journeys, too

So paint in your song, whisper into the canvas
life's dreams, hints, fears, realities, calamities, fates, resolutions
Now and then hopes and fantasies and yes even humour
Let the smiles burst forth in color and merriment or
Let it announce the day in the life of she who is consumed
in this one indulgence of expression singing worlds of sight
to the blind eyes of humanity

DONT LET THE MOMENT GET TOO BIG FOR YOU

Whether you're playing in a basketball game or
In recital playing your version of Rock's Esquisine
in V Minor or An amateur painting in the presence
of Van Gogh, Da Vinci, or Rembrandt or Performing
ballet for the first time on stage before an audience of
thousands

Its important to remain in the present and involved in your
quest
So immersed the art or skill takes precedence
Can't let the fact that you are there, steal your capacity to
deliver
Deliverance is why you are there, why you must accept the
moment

But not let the moment dominate because if the moment
controls
the craft becomes secondary and incapable of deliverance
So swallow, breathe and be expressive within every single
second available to you
Because there will come a second in which your time will be
up, as it is so often with time

Dwelling on the moment makes it too big and therefore a
monster emerges
A monster so gargantuan it swallows up the endeavor and
stalls the delivery
The delivery must be nurtured, kneaded, assuaged, chided,
prompted, kicked, pulled
Allowing absorption resulting in revelation which ultimately
leads to illumination and Deliverance...the baby is borne

38

CRUNCH

I am convinced that there is some psychological relationship between
the taste and the sound
Marketers and advertisers have capitalized on the crunch factor
The taste of it is great...whatever it is ...obviously
but there is something to the sound of it...or
maybe it's the feel of the crunch, as we munch...on
potato chips...is there any significance to the name...lays
It lays in wake for our ever constant return...frito...lays...and
the crunch is always there, just pay the fare
crunch is found in more fried foods than not...there
is the crunch of fried chicken, fried fish, fried shrimp, and french fries
un huh, while there is the taste on our tongues
our jaws hold the crunch provided by our pressure and teeth
I submit there is a connectivity between the bearing down,
grinding gears of pressure on our obvious selections which
communicates a squealing delight satisfying our
rights for salivatory
choices of rememberable recurring yearnings
for the crunch with the munch

8 YEAR OLD THUMBSUCKER

My thumb and I, we are one and the same
I walk and talk and sit and dance
and my thumb stands patiently by
Right there with me
It does not ask for pay, or love
It does not need a special circumstance to be enjoyed
It does not need to be conditioned for it has been brought up
and kneaded and nurtured, as I grew
It was brought up with me
It was one and the same
I with it and it with me

We are not understood, of course
But, we do not ask to be understood
We just ask to be left alone
on our own
Independent, self sufficient
Existing one for all
All for one
Together, when we need to be
Strong yet alone
the other for the one
Together or separate, we be

What do we need of your understanding
What do we need of your love
For we have the enjoyment of our own mutual forces
Entwined together in our mutual understanding of
Interdependence of child and thumb
Thumb and child

40

BUTTERED PANCAKES

She makes 'em from scratch
Used to sift them but found that made them too thin
Used to drop butter straight in, but couldn't taste any value

I don't know what she did to change the recipe
But them pancakes talked to me
Some say, it must have been the syrup
Others say, naw it was the hot butter stirred in again

I don't know what it was that made them things so sweet
She mixed them and stirred them only for a moments time
Turned her back to heat the skillet
I watched her throw a little water on and start a sizzle

She turned back around and that's when I saw a twinkle
It was in her left then moved to her right, she winked
Then asked, how many cakes you want today
I asked her thin or thick, cause you know it matters

Sooo she poured a little on the griddle and watched it plump
She flipped that sucker over, cocked her head and said,
This thick enough for you, I smiled and answered,
I won't know til a little taste tells me soooo

She lifted the little of the cake just for me to taste
With a tinge of butter to please my tongue
Cautioned me, it's hot don't you know and
I knew right then, this was definitely the one

Hotcakes buttered to my taste, Yummm, Yum

41

THE TORTOISE SWING

A shadow seems to dance in the moonlight

The shadow ever so graceful treated the light pole, as if it were its
partner

The shadow itself would flicker, as if it were the light itself

So intrigued was I that I climbed out of my bed to be treated to the
show

My efforts proved hollow From my vantage point

Every night I tried to be present for this show only to garner a few
moments of this rhythmic treat

So I thought, one night I will Capture this in its entirety

So I slept in my clothes and the first glimpse I had of the shadowy
dance I chose not to dawdle but to rush forth only to trip over a shell
and make sooo much noise as to wake the neighborhood and roof,
roof startle the dogs

I felt foolish certain to be more careful the next time

Me avoiding that oblong shell like thing

and the mysterious shadowy dance

Tried as I might for several nights

So much and so my sleep began to suffer

I began to fall asleep earlier and

heavier til one night I could barely

Keep my eyes open

Yet in my stupor I faintly remember a slowly moving
Tortoise
No dancing shadow to be found
Only a very round and slowly, moving tortoise peering around
Trash bins and light poles but suddenly the shell is abandoned
And low and behold the shadow emerges to the rhythmic glittering
Light in the night
It glides and rises without effort flickering with new life and
spontaneity
The tortoise without its shell has a different effervescent life

A sparkling celestiality spawned at night yet hidden from view but
for only a quiet stealth few

A light flickering all over the stage, bouncing on objects and yet
settling amongst colors, tinkling on reds, lingering in blues, jelling
in oranges, skipping in yellows, burying itself in browns,
disappearing in blacks, reflecting itself in whites, dancing in
combination colors. The light catches a swing ride like a child
pumping its legs climbing higher and higher to reach the sky. The
light comes alive with a giggle, old and young ears hear and
hearken to the sounds of joyful pleasure. The light beckons all
who hear to join in the merriment of memories for young,
intermediate and old. All cares are placed on a later shelf and
hearts race faster and faster to catch up. Catch up and join in to
that time when times moments dwell upon every single heart
like a bursting raindrop.

OCEAN WAVES

Its funny how being hit by the ocean waves makes you realize Your mortality. Oh, we try to make it fun and we often do. Ah but the water talks to you. It tells you, I am real. I emerge initially as a tiny drop but collectively, I dominate any world. I talk to you, my splashes invite you in and my song calls out, all kinds of whispers. Like you I have moods, sometimes I roar with fury. When left alone, I echo my loneliness.

Its funny how being hit by the ocean waves makes you realize your mortality. One hit tells you, I am here and you can't handle these pretty white rippling multidirectional collective surges of just water. First, sometimes cold, then warm and surroundingly sustaining. So you want to play. You want to jump, dive in, float, glide, sail and swim. Do so but know that you are within my depths whether on the surface or within.

Its funny how being hit by the ocean makes you realize your mortality. One hit can knock you over and under. Your size and weight matter, so being cautious should be your mantra. Never ever assume my ripples are safe because your confidence can come up topsy turvy. If this sounds bragadocious, hear the voice, heed the warning. My bite is sustainably worse than my roar.

Its funny how being hit by the ocean makes you realize your mortality. You don't get that sense just walking along the shore or sitting on the sidelines but trying to dance with a slow rising steadily moving mounting regular looking wave can unbalance a man weighing 235 pounds. Ocean waves don't ask or fight for respect because it is easily given rather snatched with or without dignity. Arriving in waves of giggles or surrenderous laughter and respect.

GRACE BY WAY OF JESUS CHRIST

How can you not love God
If you understand Grace
No matter how tough life gets
No matter how daunting the task

There is nothing we hope for that we cannot ask
And its not because we deserve or earned it
Its not a natural birthright, its more because of who he is
and the inherent goodness of God

How can you not love God
If you understand Grace
No matter how tough life gets
No matter how daunting the task

We were blessed from inception only because of Grace
Given despite all that I am, Given despite all I have done
A multitude of goodness washes over man and not at
his behest
Rather in spite of all that we have

COLLARD QUEENS

Collard green sculpted hips
Exclusive Deliberate guiles
Hide amidst inquisitive eyes
Enticing one's mind's eye
While a single smile teases for energetic play

Sparkly, perfectly painted fingernails tickle the inner child's side
Evoking uncontrollable, warm gut busting laughter
Reminding us of the flavors, we blend from within

Seasoning the pot of fresh collards, kale, mustards
Onion and garlic pepper that rue
Oh yes, with plenty of hot sauce, too

Even in our rich dark, light, multicolor hues of melanin
Soothing, smooth, soft skin tones encourage the adventure of
us
because our reigning purpose was defined long ago

Supplied with mama wit, early in life
Schooled on cooking, cleaning and smoozing
The significance of kindness and love
Lady behaviors and wisdom abound

Rock the head and rotate the hips
Pop those fingers to embrace the sway of a rhythmic beat
The origin of the dance is complete, yet
A little more grooving gets everyone, moving
Such nurtured hearts drive the rhythm of our families

You know, we bring the hot sauce!

WELCOME, WATER (SMILE)

Getting in the water causes laughter and chills, simultaneously
Sometimes, the water surprises you because its warm and inviting
Other times the water warns you because its chilly and repels
But the smiles and laughter you emit make your mind acknowledge, water

Water slides on your body, is absorbed into the skin and gets us wet It
entices you to frolic and attempt to hang out in this splashy playground
Stay and play, but you're not a fish and air breaths are important
So you surface, if you can, at least that's your plan

You try to tread, but the water begins to cover your head
Panic sets in, and you begin to ask is this water, my friend
Whats the answer, you take a gulp first through your mouth
But next the water begins to shoot through your nose

Must remember now, desperation is setting in, move those legs
Again and again, move those arms back and forth
Eyes wide open, look around, look around for some ground
No, land is not close, this is not dirt's reign, water ripples in your face

Today is the day, you must remember to embrace water's pace
Slow down, calm your heartbeat, and think your way through
This journey is one that requires more thought, just push away fear
In the water, anxiety cannot reign, calm is the order of the day

Relax and feel the joyfulness of this day, this child of the universe
Is like the dirt on the land, or the wind in the breeze or the dusting
snow, Like you and I, truly a member of this world, you have entered
into my playground and today, you must now know that I came to play,
too

Signed,

Water

CORNBREAD LOVE

Sprinkled in with a lot of goodness
Have you ever tasted a piece of warm cornbread
When the butter is dropped on to a hotly sliced portion
I don't know about you but just before tasting my eyes savor the image

The butter melts and runs a little
I know my eyelids, tongue the flavor first
Have you ever felt the mouth of your eyes, smile
It prompts your approach to a delightful pleasure

Some people are warm cornbread
And everyone knows who they are instinctively
They come with a special ambiance all their own
Their exuberant arrival evokes smiles and sometimes laughter

The room suddenly radiates camaraderie and interests
Think now, you know who he or she is
Have you ever met anyone that fits this description
Smoozing is now the element that lights this room

Combread warmth crumbles hearts and minds
The butter oozes through all negative thoughts
Eyes curl on the ends and evoke smiles
On the mouths similarly tickling ear tops

We look to one another because
We have the same or familiar thoughts
Of this someone who brightens the room ushering hugs
And compelling a desire for fun and laughter

Hey that's why we love them because we want what they give
We cherish and seek this thing that they bring
Every single time they arrive they bring this thing
This thing we so gluttonously seek, good times yall, good times

49

LESS IS SOMETIMES MORE

Feeling lazy some days and hungry everyday
Sometimes five times a day, teehee
Stopped at name brand grocery store
Picked up a rotisserie chicken
Not a great buy, bland to the taste but right for the effort
Gobbled to everyone's satisfaction buuuut
leftovers remained, it seemed for days

Cooking is sometimes a chore for me and maybe others
As I am less a cook, more of an experimenter
I love the gamble of the try, the what if, sooo
I create, I assemble, conjure, inject, manipulate until
I achieve something possibly edible and in this instance
Rotisserie chicken fricaseed by me

I chopped it up to make less chicken be more chicken
either for sandwiches or cracker spread
Depositing boiled eggs, pickle juice and mayo
With my salivary glands watering the synapses of my tongues mind
I began to relish tastes of raw and carmelized onion

Celery, salt, pepper, garlic powder, blend and stir
Tasting was pure delight

I smiled pleased with what I had created
Then left the room only to return later

Raisin chips, pineapple chunks, anchovies and or more
Uh Uhnn, stop I should go to the store
Blending and tasting erased the outer but not the inner smile
For while less is more sometimes in cooking
Experimenting for sure delights me with More

JUST EYE

Individualism is what makes you, you
Its not just physical characteristics
Its your life's experiences from birth to present
Preferred vanilla ice cream over strawberry
Macadamia nuts over peanuts
Television over music

And its change, I once was a television junkie
Now music brings me peace and arousal
Sometimes equally and at the same time
Other times separately, haunting

The sounds we utter, unique to just one
Sleeping sounds and utterances, again unique to one
Who we are is so exclusive to us that we sometimes are
confused

Feelings emerge and flow ever so slightly and quickly reveal
facial expressions, soooo fleeting
Only a seconds shot camera could chase the flow
How great is that?????
Likes, hates, loves, joys, laughters

Laughter is sometime chuckling, others giggably
You can laugh, so long and so hard til it becomes painful
Your side hurts and you want to stop but can't
and later remembering your hilarity makes you smile all
over again

www.ingramcontent.com/pod-product-compliance
Lightning Source LLC
Chambersburg PA
CBHW051556120626
46551CB00013B/1538